To Nick and Nikki H., my lifetime beach buddies
MB
For Eva, Iván, and Olov
JV

First US edition 2022
First published by Nosy Crow Ltd. (UK) 2021

Library of Congress Catalog Card Number 2021947330
ISBN 978-1-5362-2397-2

24 25 26 27 APS 10 9 8 7 6 5 4 3

Printed in Humen, Dongguan, China

This book was typeset in Berylium.
The illustrations were created digitally.

Candlewick Press
99 Dover Street
Somerville, Massachusetts 02144

www.candlewick.com

MOIRA BUTTERFIELD

illustrated by
JESÚS VERONA

LOOK
WHAT I FOUND
at the Beach

We're chasing waves and having fun.
Water sparkles in the sun.

Look what I found!
A curly seashell. The inside shines bright, like a pearl.

Can you also find . . .
- one shell shaped like a fan?
- two orange crabs on the sand?
- three spiral-shaped shells that look like trumpets?

There are spiky shells, smooth shells, flat shells, long shells, and shells that twist around and around.

A seashell is armor that a marine animal grows to protect itself.

Creatures such as sea snails live inside seashells. It's important to check that a shell is empty before moving it or taking it home—it could be an animal's house!

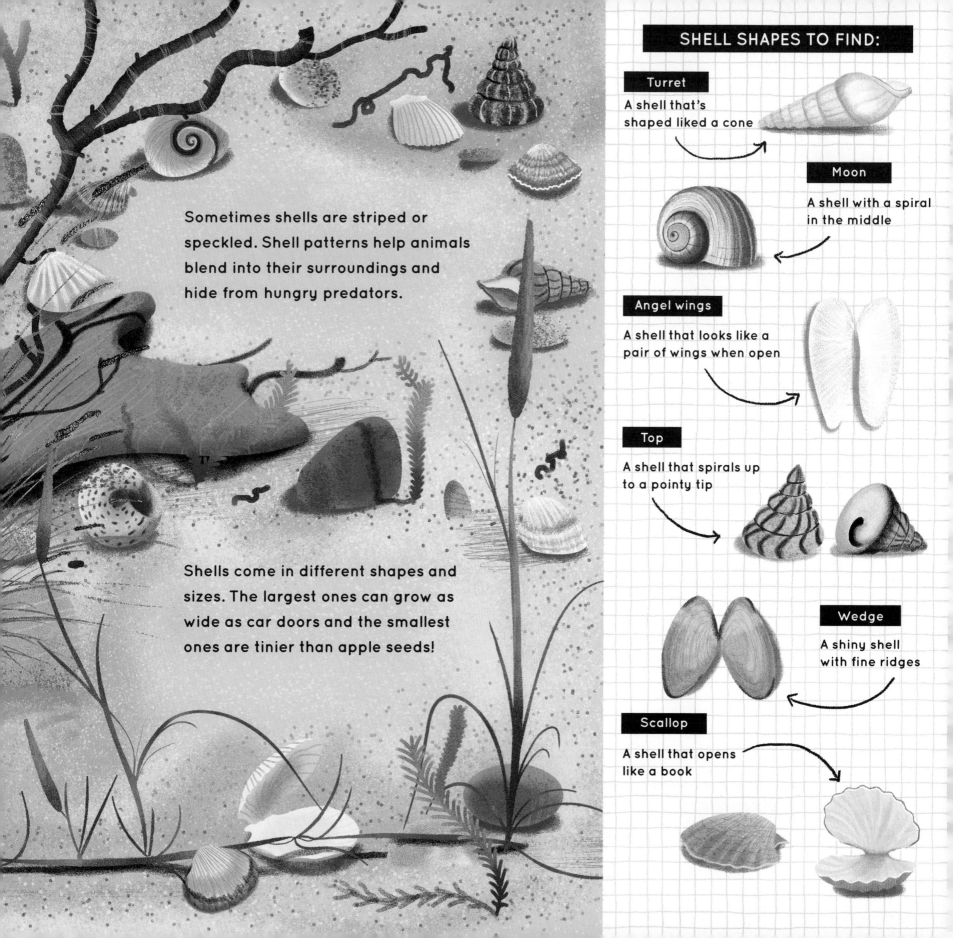

Sometimes shells are striped or speckled. Shell patterns help animals blend into their surroundings and hide from hungry predators.

Shells come in different shapes and sizes. The largest ones can grow as wide as car doors and the smallest ones are tinier than apple seeds!

SHELL SHAPES TO FIND:

Turret
A shell that's shaped liked a cone

Moon
A shell with a spiral in the middle

Angel wings
A shell that looks like a pair of wings when open

Top
A shell that spirals up to a pointy tip

Wedge
A shiny shell with fine ridges

Scallop
A shell that opens like a book

We search tide pools with a net.
Our rubber boots are getting wet!

Look what I found!
A round white pebble.
It feels smooth in my hands.

Can you also find . . .
- one speckled sea star?
- two small fish?
- three swimming shrimps?

When you hold a pebble,
you are touching something
very old. It began as rock made
millions of years ago. The water
tumbles and turns the rocks
until they are worn smooth
and small.

The stripes and spots on some pebbles are
made by different types of rock or crystal
squished together over many years, like
layers in a sandwich.

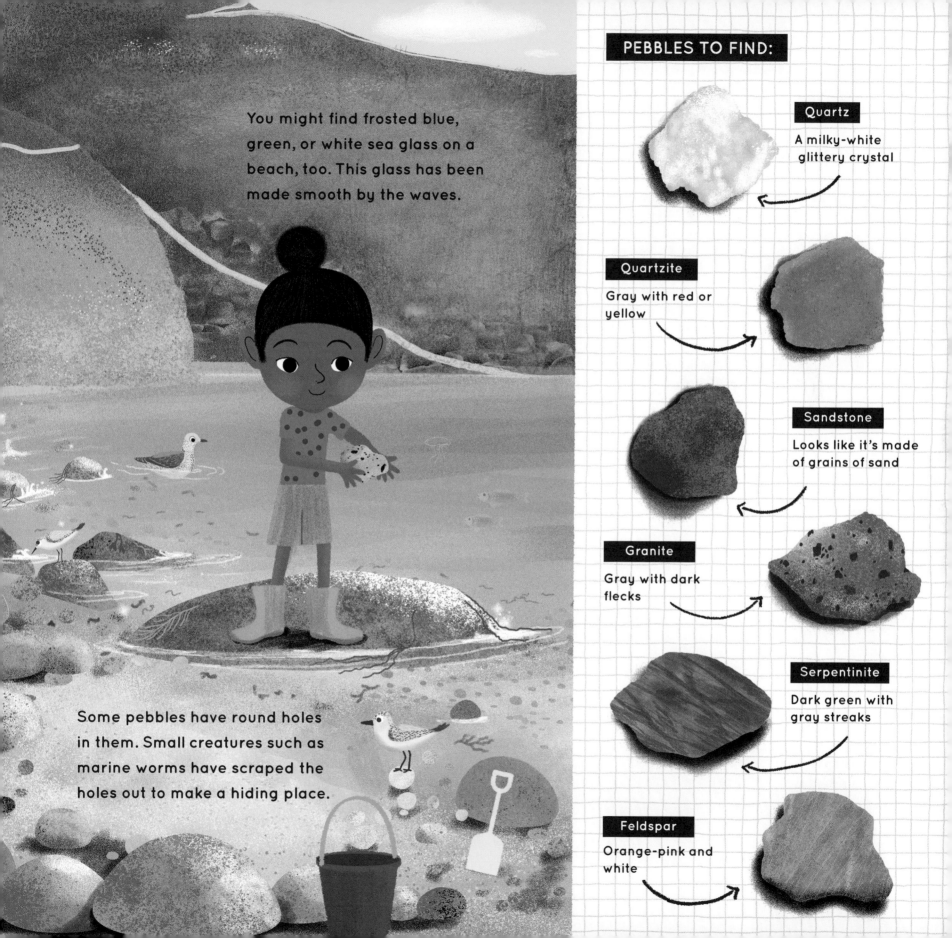

You might find frosted blue, green, or white sea glass on a beach, too. This glass has been made smooth by the waves.

Some pebbles have round holes in them. Small creatures such as marine worms have scraped the holes out to make a hiding place.

PEBBLES TO FIND:

Quartz
A milky-white glittery crystal

Quartzite
Gray with red or yellow

Sandstone
Looks like it's made of grains of sand

Granite
Gray with dark flecks

Serpentinite
Dark green with gray streaks

Feldspar
Orange-pink and white

Search the seaweed, soft and curled,
from an underwater world.

Look what I found!

An empty crab shell that
looks like an orange dish.

Can you also find . . .
- one message in a bottle?
- two seagulls looking for food?
- three different kinds of seaweed:
  red, green, and brown?

Sometimes crabs outgrow their shells,
just like how you outgrow your shoes.
Their old shells can end up on the beach
after getting washed in by the tide.

When the shell feels too tight,
the crab wriggles out from
inside. This is called molting.

A crab has a new, soft shell
under its old one. Once it
has molted, it must hide
somewhere safe underwater
while its new shell hardens.

Hermit crabs don't grow their own shells. They live inside empty seashells and move to bigger ones as they grow.

The smallest ocean crabs in the world are male pea crabs. They get their name because they are only about the size of a pea!

TYPES OF CRAB TO SPOT:

Shore

A crab with a dark green or brown patterned shell

Spider

A crab with long, spindly legs

Hermit

A type of crab that lives inside a spiral-shaped seashell

Dungeness

A reddish-purple crab

There's a cave carved out by the tide.
It's wet and dark—let's stay outside.

Look what I found!
A discarded mermaid's purse, with little hooks on both ends.
What would a mermaid keep inside?

Can you also find . . .
- one pile of stacked stones?
- two pieces of silvery driftwood?
- three limpet shells shaped like pointy hats?

A mermaid's purse doesn't actually belong to a mermaid. It's an egg case for a small shark or a skate.

The egg case has hooks that anchor it to rocks or seaweed underwater while the baby fish grows safely inside.

When the fish is ready to leave, it wriggles out of one end like money sliding out of a purse.

Mermaid's purses are found in different shapes and sizes. You might even find a big one the size of a coin purse.

Skates

A small black rectangular case

A large dark case with long horns

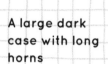

Shark

A case with curly tendrils

Up the cliff path—follow me!
There's plenty more for us to see.

Look what I found!
A fossil of a sea urchin.
It's bumpy and has a star shape on the bottom.

Can you also find . . .
- one fluttery butterfly?
- two bees busily buzzing around?
- three different kinds of coastal flowers?

Fossils are the remains of animals or plants that died millions of years ago. As the soft parts of the body disappear over time, the hard parts, such as bones or shells, turn to rock.

You might see the fossil of a plant stem or a leaf on a rock.

A sea urchin fossil has a star pattern that shows what the top of its shell looked like.

A shell fossil can be round or long; it shows the markings of the original shell.

Fossilized shark's teeth sometimes turn up on beaches. They belonged to sharks who lived millions of years ago. Some are as big as an adult's hand!

Gryphaea

Curved and with ridges, this was once the shell of a small, ancient ocean animal

Belemnite

The tip of an ancient ocean animal that is shaped like a pointy pen cap

Ammonite

A ridged, spiral fossil of an ancient ocean animal

Shark's tooth

A pointy, triangle-shaped tooth from a shark

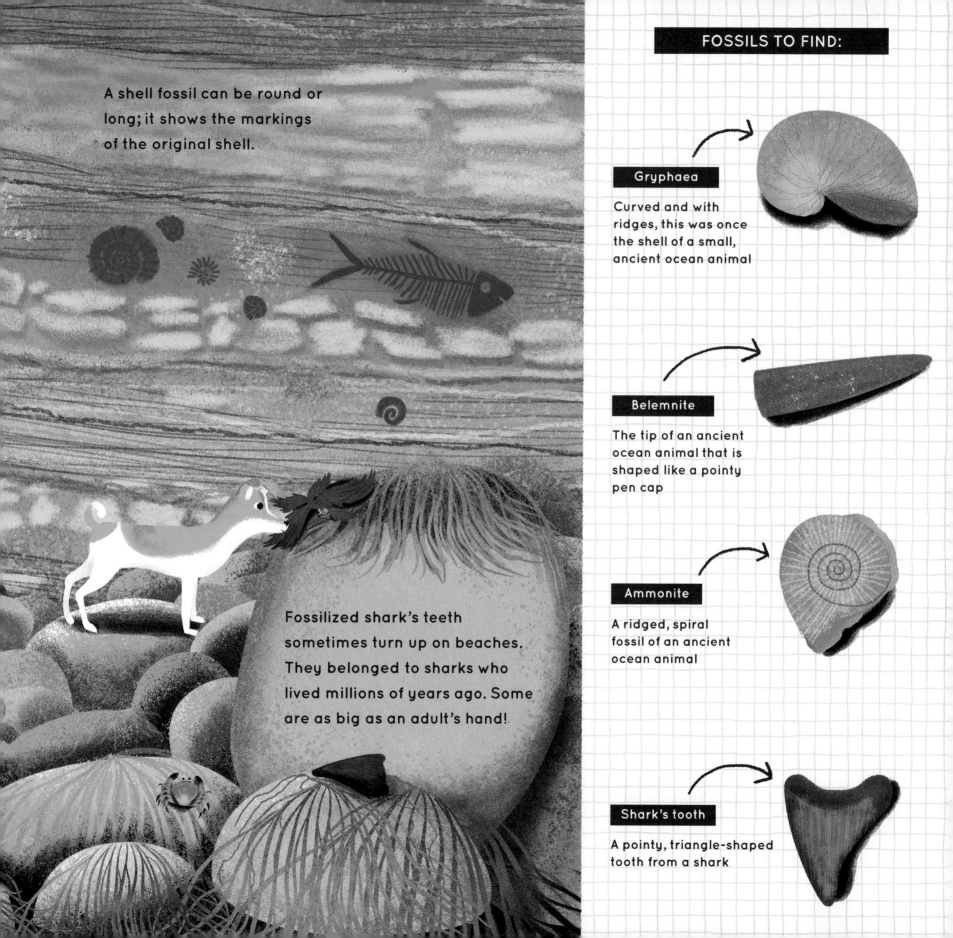

Gazing out across the bay
to ships and islands far away.

Look what I found!
A long, pointed feather shaped like a pen.
Let's pretend to write in the air.

Can you also find . . .
- One dog having fun?
- Two boats?
- Three colorful beach pails?

Feathers keep birds warm
and dry like a waterproof coat,
and they also help birds fly.

Long feathers grow on
wings and tails. Short,
fluffy feathers help keep
the bird warm.

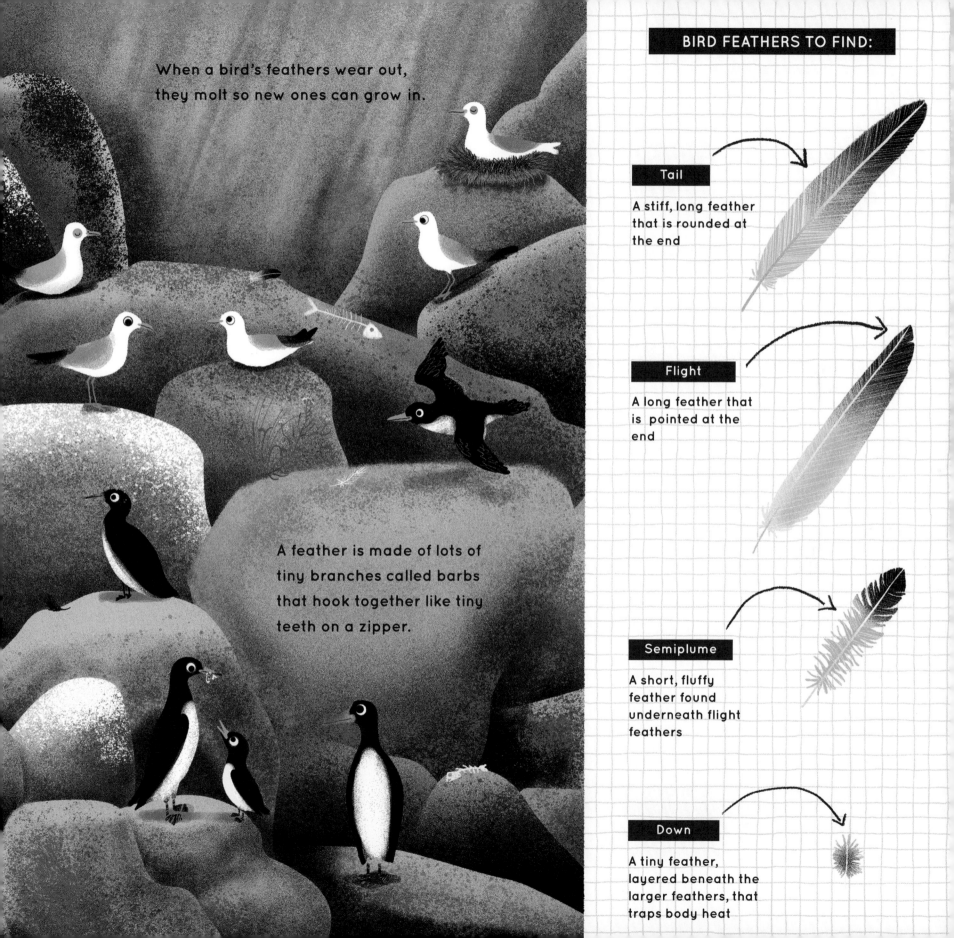

When a bird's feathers wear out, they molt so new ones can grow in.

A feather is made of lots of tiny branches called barbs that hook together like tiny teeth on a zipper.

BIRD FEATHERS TO FIND:

Tail

A stiff, long feather that is rounded at the end

Flight

A long feather that is pointed at the end

Semiplume

A short, fluffy feather found underneath flight feathers

Down

A tiny feather, layered beneath the larger feathers, that traps body heat

Goodbye, beach.
We're homeward bound.

Look at all the things we've found . . .

TREASURE!

As you collect, be thoughtful, too.
Bring no harm with what you do.

When you're exploring the beach, only collect things that have
washed up onshore, like shells or small pebbles. Always pick up after yourself
and don't leave any garbage behind. This helps ensure that the beach stays
beautiful and healthy for future visits.